Original title:
Walking with Strength

Copyright © 2024 Swan Charm
All rights reserved.

Author: Olivia Oja
ISBN HARDBACK: 978-9916-89-694-5
ISBN PAPERBACK: 978-9916-89-695-2
ISBN EBOOK: 978-9916-89-696-9

Steps Guided by the Divine Whisper

In quiet moments, I reflect,
A whisper calls, so soft, so blessed.
Each step I take, guided by grace,
In faith I find my sacred place.

The path I walk, though rugged bends,
With every prayer, my spirit mends.
The light above, it leads me on,
In trials faced, I am not alone.

The stars align in heavens wide,
With every doubt, He is my guide.
I trust the call, though blind I tread,
For in His love, I'll be well-fed.

Oh gentle heart, lead me through night,
With courage born from holy light.
I journey forth, my soul ablaze,
In sacred trust, I'll sing His praise.

I rise anew with every dawn,
A testament to love reborn.
With every breath, His will I seek,
In whispered vows, I find thePeak.

In the Shadow of His Wings, I Rise

In shadows cast, there dwells a peace,
A sanctuary where fears can cease.
With wings enfolding, calm I stay,
In God's embrace, I find my way.

The storms may rage, the winds may howl,
But in His arms, I humbly prowl.
Each tear I shed is held in grace,
In silent strength, I find my place.

Above the clouds, His promise shines,
A light that cuts through doubt's designs.
I lift my heart to skies so wide,
In trust I soar, with Him as guide.

Through trials faced, I learn to fly,
In every breath, I know I'll try.
For every fall, He lifts me high,
In love's embrace, I cannot die.

When darkness falls, His light remains,
In shadows deep, I feel no chains.
With open arms, I face the day,
In every step, I find His way.

The Conqueror's Pathway Illuminated

With faith as light, I forge ahead,
In battles fought, where angels tread.
The path before me, bright and clear,
In every struggle, He draws near.

The armor set, my spirit strong,
In sacred trust, I sing my song.
Each victory claimed, a step in grace,
In His reflection, I find my place.

The mountains high, they bow in awe,
For in His name, I heed the call.
The whispered promise, strong and true,
With every step, He walks anew.

In trials deep, where shadows creep,
His love is there, a promise to keep.
I rise as one, together blessed,
In unity, I find my rest.

The pathway winds, but I shall stand,
With heart ablaze, I hold His hand.
The conqueror's call, forever bright,
In faith, I journey towards the light.

From Dust to Destiny, We Tread

From dust we come, to dust we go,
But in between, His love will flow.
With every step, the journey grows,
In faith, our destiny bestows.

We gather strength from ancient lore,
In whispered tales of those before.
Through trials faced, our hearts ignite,
In unity, we shine so bright.

The dreams we hold, like stars they gleam,
In every heartbeat, we chase the dream.
With open hands and humble hearts,
In silent hope, our journey starts.

Through valleys low, or mountains steep,
In every tear, His promise, keep.
We rise together, hand in hand,
In faith and love, forever stand.

From dust we rise, our spirits soar,
In sacred trust, we seek for more.
With every step, our souls align,
In destiny's light, we find the divine.

Wrought of Spirit, Bound for Glory

In the silence, spirits rise,
Seeking light beyond the skies.
Hearts aflame with sacred fire,
Treading paths that never tire.

With each prayer, a bond we weave,
Finding strength in what we believe.
In the shadow, faith ignites,
Guiding souls through darkest nights.

Bound for glory, hand in hand,
Together we shall boldly stand.
Voices echo, praises sing,
In the heart, the joy we bring.

Every step a whispered vow,
Trusting grace to guide us now.
Through the storms, we shall not fold,
Our spirits shining, brave and bold.

Wrought of spirit, anchored deep,
In our hearts, the wisdom keeps.
Bound for glory, we shall soar,
Heaven's promise, forevermore.

Through Tempests Walking Boldly

When the winds of doubt do blow,
Face the tempest, let it show.
With a heart so pure and true,
Walk in faith, each step renew.

Across the waves, the journey's long,
Strength in numbers, we are strong.
Hand in hand, we rise and fall,
In His name, we heed the call.

Fears may surge like surging tide,
With the Lord, we shall abide.
In the storm's embrace, we'd stand,
Guided by His mighty hand.

Through every trial, we shall thrive,
In His love, we come alive.
With each struggle, spirits rise,
Chasing hope, our souls the prize.

Marching forth through darkest nights,
Fuelled by faith, our spirits' lights.
In the chaos, peace we find,
Heaven's truth, in love aligned.

The Call of the Brave Spirit

In the winds, a whisper calls,
Echoing through sacred halls.
Brave the heart that feels the stir,
In the silence, voices blur.

Rise up, children, take your stand,
Marching forth, hand in hand.
With each challenge, spirits soar,
In the fight, we seek for more.

Bold and fierce in faith we tread,
By His grace, our paths are led.
In the fray, the truth we share,
With each burden, love we bear.

Though the world may turn away,
In our hearts, the light will stay.
Guided by a higher call,
Together we shall never fall.

The brave spirit walks divine,
In every struggle, strength we find.
For in love, we shall persist,
In His promise, we exist.

Armor of Hope on Life's Journey

In the trials that life may bring,
Wear the armor, let it cling.
With a heart that hopes and dreams,
Trust in God's unwavering beams.

Every step on this long road,
In His name, we share the load.
Faith our shield, and hope our sword,
Onward, ever in the Lord.

When uncertainty may loom,
Let the light within us bloom.
In the shadows, dare to stand,
With His wisdom, hand in hand.

Armor shining, spirits bright,
Guided by His holy light.
Through the valleys, highs, and lows,
In His grace, our courage grows.

Life's journey may twist and turn,
But with hope, our spirits burn.
Together, strong, we shall prevail,
In the love that cannot fail.

Ascending from the Depths of Faith

In shadows deep where whispers lie,
The heart beats bold, though spirits sigh.
With each small prayer, the light breaks through,
A beacon bright, a guide so true.

From pain's embrace, we rise anew,
With faith as wings, our spirits flew.
In every tear, a lesson learned,
And from the flame, our hearts are burned.

To heights unknown, our souls ascend,
In unity, we find our friend.
Through trials fierce, our trust is strong,
Together we shall sing our song.

The Sacred Rhythm of Through the Trials

In storms of doubt, where fears collide,
We find the strength to turn the tide.
Each challenge faced, a step in grace,
In sacred rhythm, we find our place.

With every breath, we seek His face,
Through valleys dark, we run the race.
The trials teach, they mold our hearts,
In every end, a new path starts.

Through shadows cast, our spirits soar,
For in His love, we fear no more.
In trials faced, our faith ignites,
A guiding star through darkest nights.

Feet Planted Firm in Faith's Promise

With feet so firm on sacred ground,
In faith's embrace, true hope is found.
The promise sealed with every prayer,
In steadfast trust, we lay our care.

Through each storm's wake, our spirits rise,
In every heart, the light complies.
Unshaken by the world's dismay,
In faith we stand, come what may.

Our roots run deep, in Him we grow,
Through trials faced, we come to know.
With open hearts, we learn to see,
In faith's own path, we're truly free.

The Reverent Path of the Faithful

Along the path where shadows tread,
We walk in light with hearts widespread.
In every step, a prayer unfolds,
The story of love in whispers told.

With humble hearts, we seek the way,
Each moment cherished, night and day.
In reverence rare, we find our peace,
Through faith's embrace, our worries cease.

The journey's long, yet sweet the call,
In every rise, in every fall.
Together bound by love divine,
On reverent paths, our souls align.

Each Step a Prayer in Motion

With every dawn, a whispered plea,
The heart ascends on bended knee.
Each step we take, a sacred tune,
In faith we rise, 'neath sun and moon.

Through trials faced, we walk in trust,
Our souls ignited, pure and just.
A path of light, where shadows flee,
In every breath, our spirits free.

In silence found, the Spirit speaks,
In depths of heart, the truth we seek.
The journey's grace, a holy art,
In each step blessed, we take to heart.

As rivers flow to azure seas,
Our lives unfold like gentle leaves.
With love as guide, we forge our way,
In each step taken, we shall pray.

Together strong, we rise as one,
In unity, we greet the sun.
Each step a prayer, in motion's grace,
With every heartbeat, we find our place.

The Celestial Expedition of the Brave

With stars ablaze, we dare to dream,
The heavens call, a radiant beam.
We venture forth, on paths unknown,
In courage clad, our faith has grown.

Through tempest skies and shadows cast,
We seek the light that ever lasts.
The brave shall rise, from ashes born,
In trials faced, a new dawn's sworn.

Each heartbeat pulses with divine,
The universe, a grand design.
With hearts aflame, we chase the night,
In every step, we hold the light.

With angels near, we feel their grace,
The sacred dance in time and space.
From earth to skies, our spirits soar,
In faith united, we are more.

The brave shall find their sacred signs,
In every star, a love divine.
As we ascend, our souls ignite,
In this expedition, all is bright.

The Resounding Echo of the Faithful

In whispers soft, the faithful call,
Their voices rise, a sacred thrall.
The echo carries through the night,
With hope renewed, our spirits bright.

From heart to heart, a song we share,
In trials faced, we lift in prayer.
With steadfast love, we stand as one,
In every storm, we greet the sun.

The echoes dance like gentle waves,
In unity, the lost are saved.
With every note, a promise clear,
In faith we stand, we persevere.

In sacred places, hearts align,
The resounding truth, so pure, divine.
With open hands and lifted eyes,
We chase the light that never dies.

Through every trial, our voices soar,
The faithful's song forevermore.
With every echo, love shall reign,
In the heart's temple, we remain.

Path of Radiant Resilience

Through valleys deep, where shadows lie,
We press ahead, our spirits high.
With every step, a beacon shines,
In faith, we find what hope defines.

Each challenge faced, a lesson learned,
Through darkest nights, our hearts have burned.
In radiant strength, we rise anew,
With love as guide, our vision true.

The path we tread, a sacred ground,
In every pulse, resilience found.
With light ablaze, we stand our ground,
A steadfast heart, in truth we're bound.

As seasons shift, our spirits grow,
In every storm, the love will flow.
The path ahead, a sacred quest,
In trials faced, we find our rest.

With courage strong, we chart our way,
In radiant resilience, we shall stay.
Through every challenge, hearts entwine,
In faith we walk, our souls align.

The Journey With God as Our Guide

In quiet whispers, He leads the way,
With every heartbeat, we choose to stay.
Through trials and storms, our spirits soar,
Together we walk, forevermore.

With faith unshaken, we tread the road,
In moments of doubt, His love bestowed.
Each step a promise, each moment a call,
His light surrounds us, we shall not fall.

In valleys low and mountains high,
With God beside us, we learn to fly.
His hand our compass, His truth our song,
In trust we find where we belong.

Through shadows lurking, hope brightly shines,
In prayer and peace, our heart aligns.
For every step, in grace we move,
In tender mercy, we find our groove.

The journey unfolds, a sacred quest,
In every challenge, we are blessed.
With God our guide, our faith renewed,
In love's embrace, we are imbued.

The Sacred Steps of Unyielding Faith

In steadfast hearts, the seeds are sown,
A path of trust where love is grown.
With every prayer, the spirit flies,
On sacred steps toward the skies.

Through trials fierce and doubts that creep,
We hold the promise, our souls shall leap.
With courage bold, we march ahead,
In faith's embrace, we find our bed.

Each tear a blessing, each loss a gain,
Through darkest nights, we feel no pain.
For in our journey, God stands near,
Guiding our footsteps, calming our fear.

With hearts as one, we sing His praise,
In every moment, His love we raise.
On sacred ground, our spirits soar,
In unyielding faith, we seek no more.

Together we stand, in unity strong,
In faith's sweet measure, we all belong.
The sacred steps show us the way,
In every heartbeat, we choose to stay.

The Resplendent Path of Chosen Souls

Upon the road where hope resides,
The chosen souls walk side by side.
With every breath, a call to grace,
In unity found, we embrace.

With hands uplifted, hearts open wide,
In acts of kindness, our spirits guide.
Each step we take, a light to share,
For love ignites the hearts that care.

In moments fleeting, we find the truth,
With playful joy, and eternal youth.
The path is bright, though trials may daunt,
In faith's assurance, our dreams we flaunt.

With each reflection, we seek the wise,
Through prayers whispered, we touch the skies.
In fellowship woven, our bonds grow strong,
On this resplendent path, we belong.

Together we rise, our echoes sing,
In sacred harmony, our spirits cling.
On chosen paths, let love unfold,
Within our hearts, the truth we hold.

The Ascent of the Fearless Heart

In valleys deep where shadows creep,
The fearless heart dares not to sleep.
With courage rising, hope takes flight,
We journey on toward the light.

Each trial faced, a stone may fall,
With faith unbroken, we heed the call.
The mountains loom, yet we ascend,
With God beside us, love shall mend.

With every whisper of the breeze,
Our spirits climb, our hearts find ease.
In sacred trust, we seek the dawn,
Through every challenge, we carry on.

In unity strong, we forge the way,
With fearless hearts, we greet the day.
Embracing grace, we learn to fly,
Together in faith, we'll never die.

The summit beckons, our journey clear,
With love as fuel, we conquer fear.
The ascent of hearts, forever vast,
In light and love, our souls are cast.

Lifting Spirits with Each Step

With every step, I rise anew,
Guided by a light so true.
The burdens lift, the weight is gone,
In hope and faith, we journey on.

Each prayer whispers in the night,
A gentle song, a soul's delight.
Through valleys deep, my spirit soars,
Embracing love that forever pours.

In trials faced, the heart grows wise,
A sacred truth beneath the skies.
With open arms, I greet the dawn,
For every step, a grace reborn.

With hands held high, we seek the way,
In unity, we choose to stay.
A tapestry of dreams we weave,
In every moment, we believe.

So lift your spirit, take the stride,
In faith and trust, we shall abide.
Each step we take, a sacred dance,
In love divine, we find our chance.

The Quest for Divine Solace

In shadows deep, a heart does yearn,
For solace found and wisdom learned.
Through silent woods, I seek the flame,
In every whisper, call His name.

The mountains high, the rivers wide,
In nature's arms, my fears subside.
With prayerful heart, I walk this land,
In search of peace, I take His hand.

Each moment passed, a gift bestowed,
In trials faced, our spirits glowed.
Through valleys low, the path is clear,
In quiet trust, I persevere.

With open eyes, I see the signs,
In every leaf, His love entwines.
The stars above, a guiding light,
In darkest nights, they shine so bright.

So journey on, my soul's delight,
For in the quest, we find our sight.
With faith as anchor, hope as song,
In His embrace, we all belong.

Resolution Found in Life's Journey

In every breath, a choice is made,
To seek the light, not be afraid.
Through winding roads and stormy skies,
In trust, I rise; my spirit flies.

The road ahead may twist and turn,
With lessons learned, my heart will burn.
In each trial, a chance to grow,
In faith, I find the strength to know.

The journey's weight may feel so vast,
Yet in His love, I find my cast.
Each step I take, a promise deep,
In every challenge, courage steeped.

With resolve I march, my heart aligned,
In joyful praise, true peace I find.
Through hills and valleys, hand in hand,
Together strong, together we stand.

So let the journey take its course,
With faith as guide, a steady force.
In every moment, truth revealed,
A resolution, spirit healed.

The Firm Foundation of Faith's Path

On solid ground, my feet do stand,
With faith as rock, I take His hand.
Through storms that rage and winds that blow,
In every trial, His love will show.

Each step I take, a sacred vow,
To seek His grace, to learn the how.
With open heart, I greet the day,
In faith's embrace, I find my way.

The path may twist, the shadows loom,
But in His light, there is no gloom.
Each challenge faced, a lesson learned,
For in His arms, my soul has turned.

With trust as guide, we walk this road,
In every heart, His love bestowed.
Through trials deep and joys that lift,
In gratitude, my spirit's gift.

So let us build on faith's firm stone,
In unity, we're never alone.
For every step, a promise bright,
In His embrace, we find our light.

Summit Bound Through Faith's Embrace

Upon the mountain high and steep,
With faith as anchor, promise deep.
Each step we take, a prayer we breathe,
In trust we walk, our hearts believe.

Through trials fierce and storms that roar,
The light above will guide us sure.
In every loss, in every gain,
We find the strength to rise again.

With eyes uplifted to the skies,
We seek the truth where hope complies.
In silence soft, the answers come,
Our souls alight, we are not numb.

As shadows fall on paths we tread,
A whisper speaks, fear not, be led.
Embrace the journey, sacred trust,
In every struggle, rise from dust.

At summit's peak, our hearts rejoice,
In faith united, we find our voice.
For every step upon this crest,
We find our peace, eternal rest.

Guided Through the Mist of Uncertainty

In morning light, the fog descends,
Yet faith will guide where path extends.
Each breath a step upon this way,
Through whispered prayers, we find our stay.

The world may shift beneath our feet,
But love will hold, will not retreat.
In trembling moments, hearts align,
With gentle hands, the hand divine.

As doubts arise like clouds above,
Each heartbeat sings a song of love.
With every trial, a lesson learned,
In shadows cast, the lantern burned.

Through darkened nights and weary days,
We find the strength in winding ways.
For in the mist, His voice will call,
We rise anew, we never fall.

With courage born from faith so true,
The path unclear, but dreams in view.
In every step, our spirit's flight,
We walk by faith, not by mere sight.

Steps Carved in the Stone of Belief

In ancient stone our footprints lie,
A testament beneath the sky.
With every trial, our will ignites,
In faith we find our inner lights.

Each step we take, a vow is made,
In silent strength, the fear will fade.
Through valleys low and mountains high,
Our whispered hopes ascend the sky.

In trials faced and battles won,
The journey's grace has just begun.
With hearts ablaze, our spirits soar,
In every moment, we seek more.

Upon the rock of steadfast dreams,
The flowing river softly gleams.
Our paths are marked by love's embrace,
In every step, we find our place.

So let us walk, with courage bold,
In faith our stories will be told.
For in the stone of belief's bond,
We find the strength to journey on.

The Divine Compass in Every Step

A compass set within our soul,
It guides our hearts to make us whole.
With every turn in life's wide plan,
We follow Him, the Son of Man.

Through each decision, small or grand,
The path unfolds, a gentle hand.
In whispers soft, our spirits meet,
The sacred guide, in darkness sweet.

When lost amid the shifting sands,
His love will lead, our hearts in hands.
No fear shall mark the way we tread,
For in His grace, our doubts are shed.

With every mile, the promise bright,
A beacon shining, purest light.
In every step of joy or strife,
The compass points to endless life.

So walk with faith, with love in heart,
Embrace the journey, play your part.
For in each step, divinely blessed,
We find our peace, our souls at rest.

Rising with Each Sacred Breath

With each breath, I rise anew,
The spirit soars, the heart is true.
In quiet prayer, I find my light,
Guided by faith, dispelling night.

In every sigh, the world draws near,
Whispers of love chase away fear.
A pulse of grace, a timeless flow,
In sacred silence, the truth we know.

Golden rays that pierce the dark,
Embrace the soul, ignite the spark.
In every moment, chance to see,
The breath of life, our legacy.

With gratitude, the heart expands,
In sacred trust, we make our plans.
A journey born from deep within,
Awakening the joy, they win.

In every fiber, love's embrace,
Rising higher, we find our place.
With each breath, a holy quest,
In every heartbeat, find our rest.

The Arc of Journeying Souls

Across the skies, our spirits soar,
In the boundless realm, we explore.
Each step we take, a timeless dance,
With faith as guide, we seize the chance.

The winds of change, they gently sweep,
Awakening dreams from sacred sleep.
A tapestry of lives entwined,
In love's embrace, our path defined.

Through valleys deep, with burdens borne,
We rise again, reborn, transformed.
In unity, our voices blend,
Through trials faced, we find the mend.

Glimmers of grace in every trial,
A guiding hand, a loving smile.
Each rise and fall, a tale to tell,
In faith's embrace, we find our well.

Together we walk, hearts intertwined,
In every journey, purpose aligned.
With every breath, our spirits whole,
We craft the arc of journeying souls.

Grounded in Graceful Resolve

In the stillness, I find my strength,
A gentle power, a boundless length.
With faith as anchor, I stand tall,
In each moment, I'm heeding the call.

Temptations whisper, shadows may loom,
Yet in my heart, there's sacred room.
With resolve that shines, unyielding, pure,
I trust the path, of this I'm sure.

Each trial met with open arms,
In grace I move, away from harm.
With every step, a purpose clear,
In silent prayer, I banish fear.

Grounded in light, I walk with peace,
This journey's gift, a sweet release.
In every struggle, wisdom grows,
In faithful trust, my spirit knows.

Rejoice in steps that lead us home,
With hearts of love, no more to roam.
In graceful resolve, I find my place,
In the embrace of boundless grace.

Steps Cloaked in Divine Omnipresence

In every step, divinity walks,
In silent whispers, the spirit talks.
Cloaked in light, we journey on,
With every breath, the past is gone.

With faith as fire that brightly burns,
We seek the truth, the heart still yearns.
Each path we tread, the holy ground,
In sacred harmony, love is found.

Stars above in velvet night,
Guide our souls with gentle light.
In every heart, a spark ignites,
Through life's chaos, we find new sights.

With open arms, we greet the dawn,
In every trial, we're not withdrawn.
Embraced by grace, we rise above,
In every struggle, find the love.

In every moment, a chance to see,
The divine tapestry weaves through me.
Steps cloaked in presence, bright and clear,
In faith's embrace, we draw near.

Journey of the Steadfast Heart

In quiet woods where shadows play,
A heart seeks truth both night and day.
With every step, faith lights the way,
To a promise where souls will stay.

With prayerful whispers in the breeze,
Patience grows in bending trees.
Through valleys deep, in trials, ease,
The Spirit guides, our hearts appease.

Where rivers flow and mountains rise,
Each challenge faced brings about wise.
In trusting hands, our hopes surmise,
A journey blessed beneath the skies.

With worship sung and praises loud,
We walk this path, a faithful crowd.
In every moment, pure and proud,
In God's embrace, we are endowed.

And as we tread on sacred ground,
In steadfast hearts, His love is found.
For every step, His grace abound,
In the journey, we are unbound.

Steps Guided by Divine Light

In darkness deep, we find our way,
Each step ignites a bright display.
With heavenly light to guide our feet,
We walk in faith, our hearts complete.

The path unfolds like morning's gold,
With every story, truths retold.
In whispered prayers, our dreams behold,
A future bright, a love so bold.

Through valleys low, we stand in grace,
With open hands, we seek His face.
As burdens lift, we find our place,
In every trial, His warm embrace.

With joyful hearts, we rise and sing,
Our lives transformed, His joy we bring.
In every note, our spirits cling,
To the promised peace that faith can bring.

With every step upon this earth,
Our hearts ignite with boundless mirth.
In God's own light, we find our worth,
In every moment, we find rebirth.

The Pilgrim's Courageous Ascent

With feet of faith, we climb the hill,
The summit calls, our hearts fulfill.
Each step is met with hope and zeal,
A journey rich, a sacred deal.

Through storms we face, through winds that blow,
With steady hearts, His strength we know.
In every fear, our courage grows,
A guiding star, His love bestows.

As mountains tower, trials are steep,
In silent prayer, our spirits leap.
With every breath, His promise keep,
In faith's embrace, our souls weep.

When shadows darken, light shines bright,
In every step, we seek His light.
With hands uplifted in the night,
A pilgrimage of love and might.

To reach the peak where angels sing,
And hear the joy that heaven brings.
In every heart, His praises ring,
The pilgrim's path, a sacred thing.

Marching to Heaven's Call

With fervent hearts, we rise as one,
Our journey starts, the race begun.
With every stride, we seek the sun,
In faith united, we have won.

In harmony, our voices blend,
With every word, our spirits mend.
In joyful march, our hearts ascend,
To where the love of God won't end.

Through trials faced and battles fought,
We cling to grace that love has brought.
In every lesson, wisdom caught,
With every prayer, our fears are naught.

In joyful steps toward heaven's gate,
We rise and shine, defeating hate.
With arms open wide, we celebrate,
In love and light, we radiate.

As we embark on sacred space,
With heavenly love, we interlace.
In every heart, we find our place,
Marching together toward His grace.

Steps Chosen in Holy Assurance

In the shadows, we find His grace,
Guiding hearts in every place.
With each step, our spirits soar,
Clinging to the love we adore.

Whispers of hope in every breath,
A promise made beyond death.
Through valleys deep, we tread with care,
For in our souls, His truth we share.

Trusting paths not always clear,
In His embrace, we feel no fear.
With faith, we walk, a journey bold,
His warmth and light, a gift untold.

In every trial, He is near,
An anchor strong, forever dear.
Each step we take adorned in love,
Secured by mercy from above.

Serving others, hearts entwined,
In holy steps, the lost we find.
A mission bright, to heal and give,
In the love of Christ, we truly live.

The Unyielding Light of the Journey.

In the distance, a beacon shines,
A promise sweet, His love defines.
Through storms and trials, we shall press,
With steadfast hearts, we find our rest.

Each mile traveled bears His name,
In every struggle, a holy flame.
With courage strong, we rise anew,
For in His light, our faith breaks through.

Guided by angels, we ascend,
On wings of grace, our hearts defend.
Embracing peace in sacred trust,
With every step, we walk, we must.

The road is long, yet never lone,
In every heartbeat, His love is known.
Through trials faced, the spirit's song,
Reminds us where we all belong.

For in His light, no shadow stays,
Each path we tread, a hymn of praise.
As pilgrims here, we share His way,
In unity, we rise and pray.

Path of the Resolute Spirit

On this path of hope and grace,
We find our strength in His embrace.
With every choice and every turn,
In sacred stillness, hearts will burn.

Through trials faced, our spirits rise,
In faith's embrace, we find the prize.
Unyielding love guides every stride,
In humble trust, we will abide.

Whispers of truth through every night,
Transform our doubts into pure light.
With open hearts, we rise anew,
Together in His love, we grew.

As stars align in heaven's dome,
We walk united, never alone.
His gentle hand forever guides,
With peace bestowed, our hope abides.

The path we tread, a sacred quest,
In every heartbeat, find our rest.
With joyful praise, we lift our song,
On this resolute path, we belong.

Feet of Faith on Sacred Ground

Upon this sacred earth we stand,
With humble hearts linked hand in hand.
Each footstep echoes through the years,
In faith we walk, dispelling fears.

With every dawn, grace is renewed,
In every heartbeat, love's imbued.
The path is steep, the journey grand,
Yet we find strength together, hand in hand.

Through mountain high and valley low,
In His embrace, our spirits glow.
The light of hope shows us the way,
With faith, we greet each coming day.

In unity, we share this space,
Each story woven, a touch of grace.
With open hearts, we give our all,
In trust we rise, we will not fall.

So let us walk on holy ground,
In love and faith, our hearts abound.
For in this journey, we will find,
The strength of spirit, love defined.

Beneath the Wings of Providence

In shadows cast by grace above,
We find our solace, strength, and love.
With faith as armor, hearts ablaze,
We seek the light through darkest days.

Beneath the wings, we stand as one,
In every battle, we have won.
With whispered prayers, our spirits rise,
To meet the dawn with hopeful eyes.

The storms may rage, the winds may howl,
Yet in His presence, we will growl.
With every trial, a lesson learned,
A brighter path, our spirits yearned.

Each tear we shed, a sacred sign,
Of love that binds, divine design.
Together we walk, hand in hand,
In fields of grace, a holy land.

With hearts aligned, we march as one,
In the light of Truth, we will not run.
For under wings, our fears subside,
In Providence, we will abide.

Feet Firm on Sacred Soil

Upon this earth where we are bound,
Our faith like roots, in soil is found.
With every step, we tread on grace,
Each heartbeat echoes heaven's place.

We cultivate the seeds of peace,
In every man, kindness to increase.
With unity and love as guide,
In sacred soil, we will not hide.

With weary feet, we trek ahead,
Through every doubt, we shall be led.
In trials faced, our strength will show,
With faith renewed, we rise and grow.

Embrace the call, the gentle voice,
In every heartbeat, we rejoice.
With feet firm planted, spirits free,
In sacred soil, our hearts shall be.

Together we'll stand, strong and true,
In every challenge, we'll renew.
With eyes on heaven, hearts aglow,
In faith and love, we surely grow.

The Divine Footprints of Perseverance

In every trial, His footprints remain,
A guiding light through joy and pain.
With every step, we find our way,
His love surrounds, come what may.

The path may twist, the road may bend,
Yet in His grace, we find no end.
In darkest nights, His light will guide,
With every heartbeat, He's by our side.

Like rivers flow, our spirits rise,
Reflections of faith in open skies.
With steadfast hearts, we face the fight,
In perseverance, we claim the light.

For every stumble, a lesson learned,
In heart's embrace, the courage burned.
With faith as armor, we shall ascend,
To meet the dawn, on Him depend.

Forever grateful for each mile,
In every shadow, we'll find a smile.
For with His footprints, we shall stand,
In sacred trust, united hand in hand.

Spirits Unbowed, Forward We Go

In trials faced, we lift our gaze,
With spirits unbowed, through endless ways.
Together we rise, hearts intertwined,
In faith and hope, our paths aligned.

With every heartbeat, courage flows,
Through storms of strife, our strength still grows.
In unity's embrace, we find our song,
With voices raised, we shall belong.

Though mountains loom, we will not fear,
For with each step, God holds us near.
With light of dawn upon our face,
We walk with purpose, find our place.

The road may wind, but we will tread,
With hearts ignited, forward we're led.
In trials met, we rise with pride,
With faith as compass, we shall abide.

Spirits unbowed, we hold the line,
In unity's strength, our hearts align.
With open hearts and steady flow,
Together as one, forward we go.

Glorious Steps Towards Promise

In faith we rise, our hearts ignited,
With steps so bold, our path is lighted.
Through trials fierce, we find our way,
To promises bright, our souls will sway.

Each moment pure, a gift divine,
In harmony, our spirits shine.
Together we tread, hand in hand,
Towards the future, a promised land.

With hope as our guide, we face the storm,
In love's embrace, our hearts are warm.
The journey long, yet filled with grace,
In every step, we seek His face.

Through mountains high and valleys low,
With courage strong, we'll surely grow.
The sacred call, we hear it clear,
With glorious steps, we draw near.

As light breaks forth, our doubts will fade,
In trust we stand, our bond is made.
With every heartbeat, we'll proclaim,
Our glorious quest, forever the same.

The Enduring March of Grace

With every dawn, new hopes arise,
A march of grace, beneath the skies.
We lift our hearts, embrace His plan,
In unity we stand, as one clan.

Through shadows deep and fears that bind,
The light of love will make us blind.
In every challenge, faith will grow,
As seeds of grace, we gently sow.

The path may wind, yet still we tread,
In trust we move, no fears ahead.
Each step, a prayer, a voice that sings,
In gratitude, our spirit springs.

Through trials faced, our souls refined,
In mercy's arms, true strength we bind.
With every breath, we rise anew,
In the enduring grace, our purpose true.

So let us march, with joy and peace,
With every heartbeat, our fears release.
In grace we find, our spirits soar,
The enduring march, forevermore.

Relentless Pursuit of the Sacred Way

In every heartbeat, a calling clear,
A relentless pursuit, without fear.
In silence deep, our spirits soar,
On the sacred path, forevermore.

Through trials fierce and doubts that bind,
In search of truth, we seek and find.
With every step, the light we chase,
In the sacred way, we find our place.

With open hearts, our burdens shared,
In love and kindness, we are bared.
With gentle strength, we bear the load,
On the sacred road, our spirits flowed.

In unity we stand, hand in hand,
Embracing purpose, divinely planned.
Through every storm, our faith will stay,
In the relentless pursuit, we find our way.

Together we rise as one in grace,
The sacred journey, a holy space.
In every moment, let love reign,
In the pursuit of truth, we shall gain.

The Bridge of Strength Across Life's Waters

A bridge of strength across the tide,
In faith we stand, with hearts as guides.
Through raging storms and tempest's might,
With love we walk, embracing light.

The waters churn, yet we are bold,
In whispered prayers, our stories told.
Each step we take, a promise made,
On strength divine, our fears allayed.

When shadows gather and doubts arise,
We hold to hope, we reach the skies.
With every heartbeat, faith ignites,
The bridge of strength, our guiding lights.

Through valleys deep and mountains high,
We face our giants, we will not shy.
In unity, our voices sing,
The bridge of strength, our hearts take wing.

As life flows on, we hold our ground,
In love and faith, true solace found.
Across the waters, we shall cross,
The bridge of strength, love's perfect gloss.

Brave Souls in Divine Alignment

In shadows deep, their hearts ignite,
With faith as bright as morning light.
They walk with grace, hand in hand,
Brave souls united, a sacred band.

Through trials fierce, their spirits soar,
Each step a prayer, a promise to restore.
In silence strong, they seek His face,
Embracing love, a boundless grace.

In storms that rage, their voices raise,
In joy and sorrow, they sing His praise.
Together they stand, no fear to show,
In divine alignment, their spirits glow.

With every whisper and every tear,
They find His presence, always near.
Through valleys low, up mountains tall,
Brave souls shall rise, they shall not fall.

In unity, they weave the thread,
A tapestry where love is spread.
The path is clear, the journey blessed,
In brave alignment, their souls find rest.

The Harmonious March of the Believer

In cadence sweet, the faithful tread,
With hearts alight, where angels led.
They sing in chorus, a sacred tune,
Under the gaze of the silver moon.

Each step they take, a vow renews,
With every breath, the spirit views.
Through valleys dark and mountains high,
The march of faith will never die.

Hands held tight, they glide as one,
A journey shared, with grace begun.
In harmony, their voices blend,
Like streams converging, they shall ascend.

With gentle whispers, they share the way,
In love they move, come what may.
Each beat in sync, hearts intertwined,
In the harmonious march, truth they find.

They rise to greet the breaking dawn,
In every struggle, they are drawn.
The believer's path, though steep and long,
In harmony, they are forever strong.

Steppers of Purpose in the Holy Realm

They tread upon the sacred ground,
Where whispers of the divine abound.
With purpose clear and vision wide,
Steppers of faith, in Him abide.

Each footfall blessed, a journey divine,
In every heartbeat, the stars align.
Through open fields and ancient trees,
They find His presence in the breeze.

With eyes aglow, they seek His light,
In every shadow, He is their sight.
A path of grace, they dare to roam,
In the holy realm, they find their home.

Their steps are guided by love's embrace,
In every challenge, they find His grace.
With courage fierce, they march ahead,
On sacred paths, their spirits fed.

As steppers of purpose, they rise anew,
In the grand design, they see what's true.
Together they journey, forever blessed,
In the holy realm, their hearts find rest.

The Covenant of Each Sacred Step

In the stillness, a promise made,
With every step, the covenants laid.
Hearts entwined in holy trust,
In sacred bonds, we rise and must.

Through trials faced, we find our way,
Each sacred step, a chance to pray.
In whispers soft, the truth reveals,
The covenant of love, our hope seals.

Together we journey, hand in hand,
In unity's grace, we take our stand.
With faith as our guide, we walk the line,
Each sacred step, a design divine.

With open hearts, we hear His call,
In every rise, and every fall.
The sacred ties, they hold us near,
In the covenant of love, we lose all fear.

So let us tread with purpose true,
In every moment, with gratitude.
The covenant of each sacred step,
In love's embrace, forever kept.

Heartbeats in Rhythm with Providence

In stillness, I hear the call,
A whisper of hope, it shimmers small.
Each heartbeat syncs with divine design,
In rhythm with love, I feel aligned.

Clouds may gather, shadows may play,
Yet in my spirit, light finds a way.
Guided by grace, I walk with trust,
In every trial, I grow robust.

Mountains rise, and rivers flow,
Through valleys deep, my faith will grow.
With courage bold, I'll face the day,
For providence leads, come what may.

Beneath the stars, I find my path,
In moments quiet, away from wrath.
The echoes of ages sing in me,
A symphony of love, forever free.

In sacred spaces, I stand tall,
With every heartbeat, I heed the call.
In rhythm with truth, the world aligns,
In faith's embrace, my spirit shines.

The Sacred Dance of Strength and Grace

In every step, a blessing flows,
The sacred dance, in light, it grows.
With arms wide open, I sway and turn,
Embracing the strength, my spirit will learn.

Through trials faced, the lessons bloom,
In shadows dark, the light consumes.
With every twist, I'm pulled by grace,
In this divine choreography, I find my place.

The rhythm calls, my heart obeys,
In unity with the divine, I blaze.
Beyond the fear, beyond the doubt,
The sacred dance shows what life's about.

With every breath, I feel the pulse,
A force within, it starts to convulse.
Together we move, a holy song,
In harmony's arms, where I belong.

Through seasons change, I'll dance anew,
With courage born from the faith I brew.
Grace leads my steps, my soul takes flight,
In this sacred dance, I find the light.

Eclipsing Doubt with Every Step

Each step I take, I cast away,
The shadows of doubt, no longer stay.
With faith as my shield, I boldly stride,
In the light of truth, I will abide.

Obstacles rise like mountains high,
Yet in my heart, I still will fly.
For every challenge, a lesson near,
With courage steeped in love, I persevere.

Guided by hope, I soar above,
The whispers of fear, I replace with love.
Each heartbeat strong, a drum of grace,
Eclipsing doubt, I find my place.

With every moment, faith ignites,
In my spirit, the flame invites.
Through storms that roar, I'll stand my ground,
In the silence of trust, peace is found.

As dawn breaks forth, shadows will flee,
In the light of love, I am free.
With every step, I claim my right,
To walk in faith, to seek the light.

Faith as the Footing Beneath Me

In every breath, a promise held,
Faith is the footing, my spirit swelled.
On rocky paths, through the unknown,
With trust as my guide, I am not alone.

With every heartbeat, I ground my soul,
Faith lifts me high, it makes me whole.
Where darkness looms, I shine so bright,
In the depths of love, I find my light.

When doubts arise like tempests wild,
I cling to faith, my heart a child.
Through trials fierce, my spirit soars,
With faith beneath, I open doors.

In gentle whispers, truth unfolds,
Faith weaves its story, silently bold.
Each step I take, a prayer I weave,
In faith's embrace, I truly believe.

With every sunrise, I'm born anew,
In faith's firm grip, my journey's true.
With love as my anchor, I rise each day,
In the grace of faith, I find my way.

The Ascent Through Shadows of Doubt

In the night where whispers creep,
A glimmer hangs, a promise deep.
The path is fraught, with fears entwined,
Yet hope's soft glow the heart can find.

Through valleys low and mountains high,
The soul ascends, our spirits nigh.
Each step a choice, to trust the light,
Within the depths of darkest night.

A silent prayer, a gentle breath,
Reminding us of life in death.
In struggle's grasp, we learn to rise,
To seek the truth beyond our cries.

Though shadows loom and tempests roar,
We'll stand as one, united more.
For even when the doubt is near,
Our faith persists, the path is clear.

With hearts ablaze and spirits keen,
We walk the road, though yet unseen.
In faith, we find our strength anew,
Through shadows dark, we're born in blue.

Firm Feet on the Holy Terra

On sacred ground, we place our feet,
Each step a prayer, a rhythm sweet.
The earth beneath, it holds our dreams,
In nature's arms, the spirit gleams.

With hands uplifted to the skies,
We seek the truth, where wisdom lies.
The mountains echo love so grand,
A testament from nature's hand.

In gardens rich, the flowers bloom,
A promise made to chase the gloom.
With every breath, the earth we roam,
In faith we find our heart's true home.

Through trials faced, and joys embraced,
On holy paths, our fears are chased.
With steadfast hearts, we tread anew,
On Terra's canvas, pure and true.

Forever anchored, hand in hand,
We journey forth, a faithful band.
Though storms may rise, we stand our ground,
In sacred soil, our hopes abound.

Trusting the Silent Echoes of Faith

In quietude, the heart can hear,
The whispers soft that draw us near.
Through silence deep, we learn to see,
The echoes of divinity.

At dawn's first light, we bow in grace,
To trust the slow, unyielding pace.
With every heartbeat, faith aligns,
In stillness found, our spirit shines.

As shadows stretch, and daylight fades,
We linger in the holy glades.
Through every trial, the truth remains,
In silent echoes, love sustains.

The journey long, yet sweetly shared,
In faith, together, we're prepared.
Each step we take, though fraught with strife,
Is anchored in the dance of life.

We trust the path that lies ahead,
In sacred echoes, softly tread.
With hearts entwined, we walk in love,
Together here, and from above.

Beneath the Wings of Divine Support

In gentle grace, we find our way,
Beneath the wings, we long to stay.
With love encircling, fierce and kind,
In every heart, the truth we find.

Through trials faced and burdens borne,
We seek the light; we are reborn.
Embraced by love, we stand so strong,
In whispered prayers, we sing our song.

The heavens part, a guiding light,
A beacon shining through the night.
With faith as our eternal guide,
We share the path; we walk beside.

In every breath, there's strength anew,
In all we seek, we find the true.
Together we rise, unafraid,
For in His wings, we are remade.

In moments frail, we'll find our peace,
Beneath His wings, our fears release.
With hearts aligned and souls at rest,
In love's embrace, we are so blessed.

Clad in Fortitude Against the Storm

In tempest's grasp, I stand my ground,
With steadfast heart, my faith is found.
A shield of hope, my spirit's guide,
In raging seas, I will abide.

Though dark clouds loom and shadows creep,
My soul shall wake, my promise keep.
With courage strong, I face the fray,
For in His light, I find my way.

Each gust that blows, each wave that roars,
I'll trust His love, forever sure.
In battles lost, in struggles won,
The journey speaks of His great Son.

I rise anew, my heart ablaze,
In trials faced, my spirit praise.
For every storm that rages fierce,
His peace, my soul, He'll softly pierce.

Clad in His fortitude divine,
I seek His truth, my heart aligned.
In every gust, when hope seems lost,
I know His grace, I bare the cost.

The Celestial Compass of Resolve

In the night sky, a star shines bright,
A compass guiding through the blight.
With faith as pin, I chart my course,
In prayers whispered, I find my source.

Against the tide, my vision clear,
With trust in Him, I have no fear.
The heavens speak, their wisdom flows,
In trials faced, His love bestows.

Each doubt that clouds my weary mind,
I seek His light, true peace I find.
The stars align, their message clear,
In Him alone, I hold Him dear.

Through valleys low and mountains tall,
His compass leads, I shall not fall.
With every step, resolve is formed,
In grace-filled paths, hope shall be warmed.

The celestial call, my heart entwined,
In sacred trust, my life aligned.
For every dawn, His mercies break,
In steadfast love, my spirit's wake.

Grace-Filled Strides Against Adversity

With every step, His grace abounds,
In trials faced, my joy resounds.
Each burden lifted, weight releases,
In fierce embrace, my spirit ceases.

Through winding paths and rocky ways,
I walk in faith, and Him I praise.
Adversity becomes my friend,
In strength through Him, I shall transcend.

The echoes of His love inspire,
With each new dawn, igniting fire.
For every shadow that creeps near,
His light dispels, I have no fear.

In hardship's grip, I find my voice,
To trust in Him, I make my choice.
With grace-filled strides, my heart shall sing,
For in His arms, I am a king.

So forward I go, undeterred,
By whispering doubts, His truth's preferred.
In every trial, His love remains,
Through grace-filled steps, my heart sustains.

The Strengthening Tides of Faith

Tides of faith, so gentle, vast,
In their embrace, my fears are cast.
With every wave, a promise flows,
In depths of love, my spirit grows.

The currents pull, yet I stand tall,
In Him, my anchor, through it all.
With each soft swell, my heart is stirred,
His love, my compass, bliss assured.

In storms that rage upon the shore,
His strength within, I shall explore.
With every rise, each fall I'll know,
In faith's embrace, my spirit glows.

As tides recede, they leave behind,
The treasures of a heart refined.
In sacred moments, doubt will fade,
With every rise, new hope conveyed.

So let the waters freely roam,
In faith's tender tides, I find my home.
For as I trust, I learn to soar,
The waves of grace shall ever roar.

The Steep Climb of the Devout

Upon the hill, the climber strives,
With faith as gear, their spirit thrives.
Each step a prayer, each breath a song,
Through trials faced, they feel so strong.

The rocks may shift, the path may wane,
But in their heart, a holy flame.
The clouds may burst, the storms may rage,
Yet trust in Him, they shall engage.

The summit waits beyond the strife,
Where angels sing and bless their life.
In sacred whispers, answers flow,
The climb reveals the strength they sow.

With every challenge, they grow anew,
The loving guide, the path they view.
For every thorn, a petal's grace,
In every fall, the warm embrace.

At last they stand, the heights attained,
With grateful hearts, their doubts disclaimed.
The view is clear, their mission bright,
In faith, they walk towards the light.

Embracing Trials on the Chosen Route

When shadows loom, the heart must choose,
To rise in hope or to quietly lose.
With courage drawn from divine might,
They face the storms, they seek the light.

Each trial's weight is but a gift,
To forge the soul, to guide the shift.
Where thorns do prick, new blooms will grow,
In every thorn, a truth to know.

The path is steep, the road is rough,
Yet those who trust, will find enough.
With every fall, they learn to stand,
In trials faced, they'll find His hand.

With prayerful breath and faithful heart,
From trials faced, they will not part.
In struggle's clutch, they find their strength,
Each step embraced, a holy length.

And so they walk, through thick and thin,
With every burden, a chance to win.
For trials faced, they soar above,
In every struggle, they find His love.

Footprints in the Dust of Devotion

Along the path where shadows play,
Footprints lay in humble clay.
Each step a mark of faith anew,
In dust, the signs of love came through.

With every stride, the heart's intent,
In silent vows, the soul is spent.
Through barren lands and fields so wide,
In every grain, the truth does bide.

Where others falter, they press on,
A journey shared, though they feel lone.
With sacred trust as guiding star,
The footprints speak of how they are.

In whispered winds, the tales unfold,
Of sacrifices made, of hearts so bold.
In every step, the promise kept,
A faithful leap, through trials leapt.

And when the earth beneath does quake,
They stand as one, the vows they make.
For in each footprint, love's decree,
In dust of life, their legacy.

The Light Shining on the Worn Path

As twilight falls, the path grows dim,
Yet in the shadows, faith won't slim.
A glowing light, a beacon bright,
Guides weary souls through darkened night.

With every step, the heart takes flight,
In whispered prayers, they seek the light.
Though burdens weigh and doubts may creep,
In faith, the promises they keep.

When trials loom and hopes are small,
They trust the light will guide them all.
Through winding roads and ancient trails,
The Spirit's voice, it never fails.

The light surrounds, it breaks the gloom,
In every heart, it finds a room.
With open arms, the chosen stand,
Embracing love, hand in hand.

And as they walk, each step declares,
The joy of faith, the grace it shares.
For on this path, though worn it seems,
The light shines bright; it fuels their dreams.

The Sacred Circuit of the Brave

In twilight's glow, the brave do stand,
With hearts ablaze, they seek His hand.
Each step they take upon the ground,
In faith and love, their strength is found.

With prayers as shields against despair,
They journey forth through trials bare.
The sacred path, by spirits blest,
A light that guides, a holy quest.

Through valleys deep, through storms they tread,
In service true, where others fled.
Their souls aflame, their vision clear,
In every challenge, love draws near.

The echoes of the past resound,
In whispers soft, the truth is found.
For in each heartbeat, echoes rise,
A bond with heaven, never dies.

And when at last, their goal is met,
The crowns of glory, they beget.
For in the circuit of the brave,
They find the peace that none can save.

Striving on the Holy Horizon

Upon the crest of morning light,
The faithful rise, embracing sight.
With courage bold and spirits high,
They strive beneath the endless sky.

In every soul, the fire burns,
Each lesson learned, each heart that yearns.
As mountains call and rivers flow,
The path of peace, they seek to know.

With every step, their spirits soar,
In worship sweet, they long for more.
The horizon stretches, vast and wide,
Inviting all to join the ride.

Through trials faced, their hope remains,
In sacred bonds, their love contains.
With trust in God, they daily strive,
In unity, they thrive and thrive.

For every journey shares a grace,
A chance to glimpse the holy face.
Striving onward, hand in hand,
Together bound, they wander land.

The Feet of Prophets on Sacred Terrain

In lands where prophets walked before,
Their feet have trod on holy shore.
Each step a promise, deep and true,
A legacy that guides anew.

On mountains high, in valleys low,
Their voices echo, wisdom's flow.
With eyes uplifted, hearts aflame,
They call us forth to seek His name.

In sacred texts, their words inspire,
As flames of love ignite the fire.
To walk in faith, to serve the light,
To stand as one against the night.

Each soul a canvas of His grace,
In every heart, His hand retrace.
The feet of prophets, still they guide,
Through shadows dark, they stand beside.

So let us rise, with hope anew,
On sacred ground, our spirits true.
With every step, with every prayer,
We honor those who ventured there.

The Eternal Weight of Purpose

In silence deep, where spirits meet,
Awakens thoughts, profound and sweet.
The weight of purpose, heavy, bright,
It pulls us forth into the light.

Each heart ignited, sacred flame,
In service true, we lift His name.
With every task, a chance to rise,
To touch the heavens, to break the ties.

The burdens borne, they shape our fate,
In trials faced, we cultivate.
The call to justice, love, and grace,
To walk with truth in every place.

Through valleys low and mountains steep,
In faith we venture, strong and deep.
For in our souls, the echoes ring,
A symphony of purpose brings.

So carry forth this sacred weight,
With joy and passion, never late.
For in the journey, we will find,
The purpose clear, the love combined.

With Every Step, a Heart's Prayer

With every step I take today,
I lift my heart in quiet pray.
In whispered hopes, I seek Your light,
Guiding me through the long, dark night.

As mountains rise and shadows fall,
I trust in You, my Savior's call.
Each breath I take, a sacred vow,
To walk with faith, oh, Father, now.

Through storm and strife, my spirit sings,
Embraced by love, the joy You bring.
In trials faced, my soul shall soar,
For You, my Lord, I do implore.

With every dawn, renewal's grace,
Unfurling light upon my face.
In all I do, let love abound,
In every step, Your peace is found.

So guide my path, oh Lord, I plead,
With every thought, in every deed.
Let faith arise, and fears depart,
With every step, a humble heart.

Through Valleys Strong and Deep

Through valleys strong and shadows deep,
I tread with faith, my heart to keep.
In darkest hours, I seek Your grace,
A steadfast love in every place.

With weary feet, I march along,
In silence found, I hear Your song.
Each trial faced, a stepping stone,
In whispered prayers, I am not alone.

The road is long and fraught with pain,
Yet in this journey, joy remains.
For every struggle, I will grow,
With trust in You, my spirit glows.

Beneath the stars, my soul is bare,
Yet in my heart, I feel You near.
Through valleys wide, Your love shall shine,
In darkest hours, Your light divine.

So let me walk, dear Lord, with pride,
Embracing hope, You are my guide.
Through valleys strong and trials steep,
In every breath, Your promise deep.

The Faithful Wanderer's Quest

The faithful wanderer moves forth,
In search of peace, in quest of worth.
With every footstep, prayers arise,
A journey marked by sacred ties.

The path is worn, yet still I roam,
In fields of grace, I find my home.
With eyes uplifted to the sky,
I walk in love, with trust, not why.

Beneath the sun and shade of trees,
I listen close to gentle breeze.
In all the trials that I face,
I find Your strength, Your sweet embrace.

Each step a hymn, each breath a chant,
In all I seek, my heart's sonnet.
The faithful wanderer's quest unfolds,
In every story of love retold.

Though storms may rage and shadows loom,
With faith, I rise, dispel the gloom.
For on this path, I know I'm blessed,
In every moment, I find my rest.

Halos of Strength along the Way

Halos of strength along the way,
Illuminate the path I stray.
In trials faced, I stand with grace,
For You, my Lord, I seek Your face.

With every burden, You provide,
A gentle hand to be my guide.
In every step through joy and fear,
Your love surrounds, Your voice I hear.

When doubt creeps in with shadows cast,
I hold onto the truth steadfast.
For in the light of love divine,
I find my courage, I find my sign.

Through every storm and raging sea,
You are the peace that comforts me.
Halos of strength, a guiding star,
Leading me home, no matter how far.

So let me walk, O Lord, with ease,
Embracing hope upon the breeze.
With halos bright, I find the way,
In every moment, come what may.

Solemn Marches Under Heaven's Gaze

In the stillness of dawn, I tread,
Upon this path where angels led.
I whisper prayers to the sky,
For in my heart, the spirits fly.

The clouds part softly, light enshrines,
Each step a dance, a sacred sign.
Beneath the arch of heavens wide,
With faith and hope, I shall abide.

The echoes of the faithful call,
In silence deep, I stand tall.
Graced by words of love and light,
I march with all my soul's true might.

With every heartbeat, I ascend,
In solemn prayer, my heart will mend.
For heaven's gaze, it rests on me,
In this grand march, my spirit free.

The journey lengthy, yet divine,
I walk with purpose, sacred sign.
Each step a promise, a vow bestowed,
In solemn marches, I find my road.

Threads of Grace Beneath My Feet

In gentle whispers, grace is spun,
A tapestry of love begun.
Threads of mercy weave my way,
Guiding me through night and day.

With every footfall on the ground,
In sacred moments, joy is found.
These threads of grace, so soft, so bright,
Illuminate my path with light.

Through trials faced, I stand serene,
Each step a beat in this great scheme.
The fabric of my life unfolds,
In quiet strength, my spirit molds.

Beneath my feet, the blessings flow,
In grace, I find the strength to grow.
A gift bestowed, a promise kept,
In threads of love, my soul is swept.

As seasons change, the colors blend,
These threads entwined shall never end.
With gratitude, I tread this earth,
In every step, I find my worth.

Pathways Infused with Sacred Power

Upon these paths, where shadows fade,
A sacred presence serenade.
Each corner turned, a spirit's dance,
Unfurling life in every chance.

The trees they whisper tales of old,
Through timeless roots, the truth is told.
In daytime's light or moonlit night,
These pathways shine, a guiding light.

Embracing strength from realms above,
I walk in faith, embraced by love.
With heart ablaze, I journey forth,
To seek the essence of my worth.

In every stone and every leaf,
I find a story, share my grief.
These sacred roads, they hold the key,
To mysteries of eternity.

And as I walk, I feel the power,
Of every dawn, of every hour.
With open heart, I claim this grace,
In sacred pathways, I find my place.

A Soul's Unyielding Odyssey

Through valleys deep and mountains high,
A soul embarks beneath the sky.
With every step, a journey starts,
In faith's embrace, I mend my parts.

Each stumble met with grace anew,
The lessons learned, the wisdom grew.
In shadows cast, I seek the light,
With courage fierce, I rise and fight.

The stars above my guide and friend,
A cosmic force that will not end.
In quiet moments, I reflect,
On love and life, I deeply connect.

Through trials faced, my spirit climbs,
In every pulse, I mark the times.
A tapestry of dreams evolved,
In sacred truth, my heart resolved.

For in this odyssey profound,
A deeper meaning shall be found.
With open arms and steadfast heart,
A soul's true quest, it shall not part.

The Holy Path of Resilience

On the road where shadows lie,
With faith as wings, we learn to fly.
Each stone a test, each turn a grace,
In every trial, we find our place.

Through storms that rage and nights so deep,
The heart awakens, the spirit leaps.
In prayer's embrace, we gather strength,
With hope our guide, we journey length.

The weight of burdens we hold so tight,
Finds healing in the morning light.
For every tear that graces our face,
Is but a step towards His embrace.

So let us march with courage bold,
Through valleys low and pastures gold.
Each moment sacred, a lesson learned,
As love ignites, our souls are burned.

With hearts entwined, we tread this ground,
In every heartbeat, His love is found.
Rejoice, dear soul, we walk as one,
The Holy Path, our race begun.

Soulful Strides Through Faith's Garden

In the garden where hope blooms wide,
We take each step with love as guide.
Through fragrant paths and colors bright,
We dance in joy, we bask in light.

Each prayer we weave, a flower's grace,
Filling the earth with our embrace.
In unity, our voices sing,
With every note, the angels ring.

The soil nurtured by kindness sown,
Through faith's embrace, we've all grown.
With every challenge, we rise anew,
United together, pure and true.

As seasons change, with grace we bend,
In trust, we walk, no need to pretend.
Our spirits dance, like leaves on air,
In faith's garden, we find our care.

So take my hand, let's wander far,
Through sacred lands, where blessings are.
With hearts ablaze, our path divine,
In Soulful Strides, our souls entwine.

The Fortress Beneath Each Step

Upon this ground where trials lay,
We build our fortress, come what may.
With every stone, our faith withstands,
The storms of life, its guiding hands.

Each step we take, a promise strong,
In love's embrace, where we belong.
Through darkest nights and brightest days,
Our fortress stands, in countless ways.

With courage firm, our hearts aligned,
In whispers soft, His will we find.
Together bound, we face the fight,
In unity, we stem the night.

The walls we raise, in prayer and song,
A sanctuary where we belong.
With faith as armor, hope as shield,
Our fortress strong, we shall not yield.

So here we stand, in spirit's grace,
A bulwark built that time can't erase.
With every heartbeat, we forge ahead,
The Fortress Beneath, in Him we tread.

Onward Through Trials Blessed

Through trials faced, our spirits soar,
With love unwavering, we seek for more.
Each challenge met, a chance to grow,
In faith's embrace, our lights will glow.

As shadows creep, we hold our ground,
In whispered prayers, His voice resounds.
Each step we take, though steeped in pain,
Brings forth the harvest, life's sweet gain.

In moments dark, we find the light,
Through trusting hearts, the path feels right.
For every tear that stains the earth,
Is but a seed of hope and rebirth.

Together bound, we lift our eyes,
In fellowship, our spirits rise.
Onward we march, with hope ablaze,
Through Trials Blessed, our hearts upraise.

Let courage guide and faith refine,
With love as compass, we intertwine.
Onward we go, hand in hand,
In life's embrace, we take our stand.

Strengthened by the Breath of Heaven

In whispers soft, the angels sing,
A gift of grace, the heart takes wing.
With every breath, a promise clear,
Strengthened by love, we cast our fear.

Through shadowed paths and trials vast,
In faith we forge, and hold steadfast.
The light above, it guides our way,
Illuminates the dawn of day.

When storms arise and seas roar loud,
We'll find our strength within the shroud.
A shelter formed from hope divine,
In unity, our souls entwine.

Each prayer a thread, we weave as one,
A tapestry of love begun.
With hearts ablaze, our spirits rise,
Strengthened by the breath of skies.

Following the Footprints of the Wise

In wisdom's glow, the footsteps lead,
A path of light, the heart shall heed.
Each stride in faith, a seed is sown,
We gather strength, we are not alone.

From sages past, their voices call,
In stories told, their truths enthrall.
With open hearts, we seek and learn,
In every page, the lanterns burn.

In quiet moments, we reflect,
On choices made, and paths select.
With every test, we grow in grace,
Following the wise, we find our space.

Their footprints mark the sacred ground,
In reverence deep, our hopes are found.
With courage fierce, we journey forth,
In wisdom's arms, we know our worth.

Chosen Path Beneath Celestial Skies

Beneath the stars, our dreams take flight,
A chosen path, embraced by light.
In every step, the heavens guide,
With grace and love, we walk with pride.

The moonlight bathes our weary souls,
In cosmic dance, the spirit rolls.
With every sigh, the universe breathes,
In harmony, our fate it weaves.

Through trials faced, we find our way,
With faith as lantern, night turns day.
In unity, our voices rise,
Together bound beneath the skies.

Each star a dream, each wish a prayer,
In sacred trust, we lay our bare.
The chosen path, a journey grand,
In celestial grace, we take our stand.

The Pilgrimage of the Undaunted Spirit

With hearts ablaze, we roam the earth,
In search of truth, we find our worth.
An undaunted spirit, bold and free,
We rise above, in unity.

Through valleys low and mountains steep,
In every step, our promise keep.
With every dawn, a chance anew,
The light within will carry through.

When darkness falls and shadows creep,
We'll stand as one, our vigil keep.
In quiet strength, we gather near,
The pilgrimage we hold so dear.

For in the struggle, faith takes shape,
With every breath, a brand new escape.
Together, bound, we find our song,
The pilgrimage of souls so strong.

Steps of Faith's Embrace

In shadows deep, we walk as one,
Faith like the morning sun.
Each step we take, His love reveals,
Hope in our hearts, our spirit heals.

With trembling hands, we lift our gaze,
Through trials faced, in Him we praise.
Together bound, through storm and strife,
In faith's embrace, we find our life.

The road is long, yet not in vain,
For every loss, He knows our pain.
In whispered prayers, His voice we hear,
Guiding our steps, dispelling fear.

So let us rise, with strength anew,
In faith's embrace, we journey true.
Hand in hand, we share the load,
Together walk this sacred road.

The Pilgrim's Resilient Path

Upon the hill, the path is steep,
Yet onward still, I take each leap.
With courage strong, I face the night,
For in the dark, shines His light.

Through valleys low and mountains high,
My heart will sing, my spirit fly.
With every trial, my soul refined,
In the embrace of the Divine.

Each step I take, a promise made,
In faith I walk, I am not afraid.
The pilgrim's way, though rough and wide,
Is filled with grace, my constant guide.

With every breath, I seek His face,
In love's embrace, I find my place.
Through paths unknown, my heart takes flight,
For I am wrapped in holy light.

In the Light of Divine Guidance

When clouds arise and hopes seem lost,
In trials faced, I count the cost.
Yet in the dark, His light breaks through,
A beacon bright, forever true.

Each dawn I wake, I seek His will,
In silence deep, my heart be still.
His gentle voice, a soothing balm,
In storms of life, it whispers calm.

Through winding roads and distant shores,
He opens wide the endless doors.
In every chance, a chance to see,
The path He wove, laid out for me.

With grateful heart, I walk in trust,
For in His love, I rise from dust.
In the light of grace, I find my way,
Guided by faith, come what may.

The Journey Clad in Courage

With armor bright, I face the dawn,
Each battle fought, I carry on.
In faith I stand, in love I strive,
For through the dark, my soul's alive.

Every wound a tale to tell,
In storms of doubt, within my shell.
Yet through the pain, a strength is born,
In every trial, my spirit's sworn.

Clad in courage, I make my way,
Through fields of grace, and shadows gray.
His hand supports, my trembling heart,
For in His plan, I play my part.

With every step, I choose to rise,
A heart aflame, beneath the skies.
In every breath, His love resounds,
The journey's rich, in Him, I'm found.

The Journey Beyond the Valley of Shadows

In shadows deep, the heart takes flight,
A whisper calls, guiding through night.
With faith as light, on paths we roam,
To find the grace that leads us home.

Each step we take, a solemn prayer,
In valleys low, our spirits share.
Together bound by hope we rise,
To see the dawn, embrace the skies.

The shadows fade, our fears retreat,
In love's embrace, we find our feet.
The journey long, yet sweet the pace,
For in our hearts, we know His grace.

Though trials loom and storms may roar,
The strength we seek, it lies in more.
With every breath, we sing His name,
Our lives transformed, forever changed.

So onward go, with open hearts,
In unity, we play our parts.
Beyond the vale, we seek the light,
In His embrace, we find our sight.

The Woven Tapestry of Bold Hearts

In threads of faith, we intertwine,
A tapestry of love divine.
Each heart a part, each soul a thread,
In unity, our spirits fed.

With colors bright, our stories blend,
Through trials faced, we learn to mend.
In woven dreams, our hopes take flight,
Together strong, we face the night.

For courage blooms where fears reside,
In boldness found, we cannot hide.
With every stitch, new strength we gain,
In fellowship, we break the chain.

So journey forth, with heads held high,
In kindness shared, our spirits fly.
Through joy and pain, our souls connect,
In love's embrace, we find respect.

As one we stand, a radiant hue,
In grace we thrive, forever true.
A woven tale, of hearts so bold,
In harmony, our fate foretold.

Steps Anchored in Eternal Hope

In mornings bright, with eyes uplifted,
We take our steps, in faith we're gifted.
Anchored firm in hope's embrace,
We journey forth, we seek His face.

With cada paso, our spirits soar,
In trials faced, we yearn for more.
Eternal hope, our guiding star,
In darkest times, we know who we are.

The road is long, yet hearts are bold,
With every step, new stories told.
Together standing, hand in hand,
In love's great name, we make our stand.

Through valleys low and mountains high,
In faithful trust, we will not sigh.
For hope endures and love will guide,
In every tear and every stride.

So journey on, with spirits bright,
In every moment, find the light.
For hope will lead, as hearts unite,
In joy and peace, we share our flight.

The Choir of Feet Moving Forward

With every step, a song resounds,
A choir formed on holy grounds.
In harmony, our feet we raise,
To praise the path with endless praise.

Each footfall echoes love's sweet call,
In unity, we stand not small.
Together bold, our voices soar,
In every heart, we long for more.

The rhythm flows, our spirits blend,
On journey long, there's no true end.
In every stride, a truth we find,
Our echoes strong, our hearts aligned.

So forward move, through joy or pain,
In faith we trust, in hope we gain.
The choir swells, our hearts in tune,
In every dusk, we seek the moon.

And though we falter, lose our way,
In love's embrace, we choose to stay.
With every step, a promise clear,
We walk in light, we walk in cheer.

The Sacred Trek of the Brave

In shadows deep, we walk our way,
With faith as light, we find the day.
Each whisper sung, a guiding star,
The heart ignites, no fear to mar.

Through valleys low, on mountains high,
We climb as one, beneath the sky.
With courage strong, we seek the truth,
In every step, we find our youth.

A path of grace, with trials near,
We hold the hope, we cast out fear.
For every tear, a blessing sown,
In sacred bonds, we're not alone.

The morning sun, our banner raised,
With hearts aflame, we stand amazed.
The journey long, yet spirits soar,
In love divine, we seek much more.

So hand in hand, we face the dawn,
For in our hearts, the love lives on.
In every step, the brave shall tread,
With faith's embrace, we forge ahead.

Steps Carved in Divine Promise

Each step we take, a promise bright,
In valleys deep, we seek the light.
Through trials faced, our hearts align,
In whispers soft, His love divine.

The road is long, the path unclear,
Yet with each breath, we hold Him near.
Through tempests wild, He calms our soul,
In sacred trust, we find our whole.

The mountains rise, the rivers flow,
In sacred steps, His grace we know.
With every fall, we learn to rise,
In faith renewed, we touch the skies.

In search of peace, we journey far,
With humble hearts, we bear His scar.
The echoes call, we hear them clear,
In every prayer, He draws us near.

So onward we go, with hearts ablaze,
For in His light, we sing His praise.
Each step a bond, each breath a hymn,
In stepping forth, we trust in Him.

Strength Found in Every Footfall

In every footfall, strength we find,
Through trials faced, we are refined.
With faith as firm as ancient stone,
In whispered prayers, we are not alone.

The path before, a sacred trial,
Yet with each step, we wear a smile.
In struggles borne, we gain our might,
For in the dark, He is our light.

The burdens shared, our spirits rise,
With every challenge, the soul complies.
In holding fast, our hearts unite,
Together we climb, guided by light.

The echoes of faith in every land,
In unity strong, we take our stand.
With voices bold, we lift our song,
In every step, we all belong.

Through valleys deep and mountains steep,
In sacred trust, His promise we keep.
For in each footfall, love is clear,
With every stride, we draw Him near.

The Guiding Hands of Providence

In the dawn's embrace, we seek the way,
With guiding hands, we choose to stay.
Through every storm, those hands provide,
With gentle strength, we shall abide.

Through trials faced, our spirits soar,
In every heartbeat, we seek much more.
As shadows fall, He lights the path,
With trust unwavering, we escape wrath.

From mountain tops to valleys low,
The hands of grace will ever flow.
In every touch, a love profound,
In sacred paths, our faith is found.

So let us walk, hand in hand,
With hearts united, we take our stand.
In every moment, His love expands,
With guiding hands, He leads our plans.

With each new dawn, we rise anew,
In every trial, we grow and pursue.
For In His grace, we find our home,
With every step, together we roam.

A Journey Through the Spirit's Will

In the silence, the heart finds grace,
Guided by whispers of the sacred place.
Each step forward, a prayer in motion,
Flowing like rivers, deep as devotion.

Mountains loom, and valleys unfold,
With faith as our compass, we grow bold.
The path may wind, yet the spirit's light,
Illuminates shadows, turns darkness bright.

Gentle breezes carry the songs of old,
Stories of courage, in each heart told.
We tread on soil blessed by the divine,
In every heartbeat, a sacred sign.

Through trials faced and burdens shared,
In every struggle, the spirit cared.
A journey not taken alone, but embraced,
In the depth of our souls, we find our place.

Together we rise, hearts intertwined,
Fulfilling the purpose that faith designed.
Each moment a gift, each breath a thrill,
We walk united, through the Spirit's will.

Echoes of Valor in Every Stride

When dawn breaks, the faithful arise,
With courage ignited beneath endless skies.
Each footstep echoes the strength we bear,
In the face of challenges, we rise with prayer.

The wind carries whispers of saints long past,
Their deeds of valor, forever will last.
In the tapestry of faith, we weave our thread,
In unity bound, where all fears are shed.

Through valleys low and mountains high,
With a solemn heart, we reach for the sky.
The spirit within us, relentless and free,
Guides our journey, as faith's legacy.

Each heartbeat a testament of love's embrace,
In trials of life, we find our place.
With hope as our anchor, steadfast and bright,
We walk on, empowered by the light.

In echoes of valor, our souls ignite,
Together we march, facing the night.
For every stride bears witness to grace,
In the journey of faith, we find our space.

Sturdiness Under Heaven's Design

In the arms of the earth, we forge our way,
Hand in hand, we pray and stay.
With grounded hearts and spirits aligned,
We journey forth, by love defined.

The stars above twinkle with hope,
Guiding our steps, as we learn to cope.
In faith, our roots sink deep and wide,
Finding strength in the life we abide.

In moments of doubt, we rise with might,
Clinging to promises, shining bright.
As seasons change and trials test,
In heaven's design, we find our rest.

Mountains bow down, and oceans part,
In the work of creation, we each play a part.
With sturdy hearts, we face the night,
Trusting in love, embracing the light.

Through storms we weather and fears we face,
Finding solace in the sacred space.
Together we stand, in faith we thrive,
Under heaven's design, we come alive.

The Resolute Soul's Pilgrimage

In the journey of life, the soul takes flight,
With a heart unwavering, guided by light.
Step by step, through trials we move,
With each beat, our spirit improves.

The path is paved with blessings divine,
In every challenge, the truth we find.
With steadfast purpose, we rise each day,
In the strength of our faith, we find our way.

With open hearts and courage anew,
We carry the message of love so true.
Every sorrow and joy intertwine,
In the tapestry woven, our lives combine.

As we walk this pilgrimage, hand in hand,
Connected in spirit, united we stand.
Through every triumph and every fall,
In the grace of the journey, we embrace it all.

The resolute soul, on a quest for peace,
With wisdom from ages, our burdens cease.
Together we wander, with faith as our guide,
In the heart of the journey, love will reside.

Spirit's Voyage Across the Wilderness

In the blaze of the morning sun's glow,
Wander souls tethered to the flow.
Through valleys deep, where shadows dance,
They seek the light, a sacred chance.

Among the whispers of ancient trees,
Their hearts aflame, carried by the breeze.
With each step, a story unfolds,
In the wilderness, a truth retold.

Mountains high, where eagles soar,
The spirit cries out, forevermore.
Through trials fierce, and storms that rise,
Hope's gentle beacon lights the skies.

In twilight's embrace, they find their peace,
A voyage blessed, their fears release.
As stars appear, like eyes of grace,
They walk in faith, embraced by space.

A journey woven in the thread of night,
With every breath, they sense the light.
Across the wilderness, hand in hand,
They carry forth, a faithful band.

A Sacred Journey of the Unbroken

Born from trials, the spirit ignites,
In the depths of shadows, it finds the light.
With every heartbeat, a promise made,
A journey begins, with love displayed.

Through turbulent seas and desert sands,
Guided by faith, they understand.
Each step forward, a divine embrace,
Together they wander in this holy space.

The rivers they cross, the mountains they climb,
In unity forged, beyond space and time.
Their souls united, never apart,
A sacred journey, a beating heart.

In valleys of doubt, where hope seems lost,
They carry the fire, no matter the cost.
With arms open wide, they face the unknown,
For in love's embrace, they are never alone.

The road may be long, the night may seem dark,
Yet within their spirits, resides the spark.
With grace as their compass, they rise above,
A sacred journey, anchored in love.

The Trail Marked by Grace

Upon the earth, where silence weeps,
A whisper of grace in the heart that keeps.
Footsteps echo on the trail of time,
Carved by the faithful, a sacred rhyme.

Each stone a testament, each leaf a sign,
Lost in the forest, where souls entwine.
In the gentle breeze, the spirit sings,
A melody sweet, a chorus of wings.

Through fields of sorrow, through nights of despair,
They walk with purpose, their burdens laid bare.
For in every struggle, a lesson is born,
With grace as their guide, they face the dawn.

Bound by conviction, and hearts that heal,
They gather the strength in the love they feel.
A tapestry woven with threads of light,
Together they stand, emboldened by night.

The trail may be winding, the path not so clear,
Yet every summit brings joy near.
With grace as their lantern, they move ever on,
The trail marked by love, from dusk until dawn.

Hoofprints on the Path of Hope

On the dusty road where silence reigns,
Hoofprints of courage break the chains.
Each mark upon the earth they bring,
A testament to the heart's true spring.

Through valleys of shadows, they tread with grace,
With lifted spirits, they find their place.
The path may twist, the winds may blow,
Yet hope remains, a steady glow.

With every gallop, they chase the dawn,
Filling the air with a hopeful song.
In fields of dreams where faith takes flight,
They ride towards an everlasting light.

In the moments fleeting, when doubts invade,
The hoofprints linger, undeterred, unfrayed.
For every journey holds love's embrace,
And every step taken is marked by grace.

In the distance, the horizon calls,
With whispers of promise, where the spirit enthralls.
Through trials met and victories struck,
The path of hope shines, forever unstuck.

Milton Keynes UK
Ingram Content Group UK Ltd.
UKHW020042271124
451585UK00012B/998